terra magica

Edited by Hanns Reich

Translated and adapted
from a text by Ulrich Klever

Hill and Wang New York

A division of Farrar, Straus and Giroux

Dogs

Published in the United States of America by
Hill and Wang, a division of Farrar, Straus and Giroux, Inc.
ISBN: 0-8090-2044-0
Library of Congress catalog card number: 73-81578
Published simultaneously in Canada by
Doubleday Canada Ltd., Toronto
Production Office: Rudolf P. Gorbach, Munich
Manufactured by Ludwig Auer, Donauwörth
Printed in Germany

There has always been a special affinity between dogs and people; intelligence, adaptability, and devotion have made the dog man's ready helper and constant friend.

In the beginning, when canines romped around the campfires of primitive man, they served as watchdogs and ferreters of wild game. Few breeds existed then, but, changes in food, climate, and breeding habits over the centuries, caused new ones to evolve.

Eventually, dogs were tamed and bred selectively for characteristics most useful and pleasing to man. They learned to perform various tasks. Some became adept at herding sheep and cattle; others emerged as man's powerful ally in the hunt. Sturdy breeds were harnessed to carts or taught to pull Eskimo sleds across the snow. High in the Alps, shaggy St. Bernards rescued travelers lost in the storm, while at the shore huge Newfoundlands bounded into the surf to save the floundering swimmer. Bloodhounds were used to track down fugitives, and German shepherds became fierce guardians of property and man.

Not only have dogs worked for man, they have served as status symbols: the more massive, miniature, or rare a dog, the more important his master. The pug, valued as clever and saucy, was once the favorite lap dog of kings and nobles; other breeds – terriers, Chihuahuas, Pomeranians, and poodles – have also had their day in court, as favorites of the wealthy classes. In dog shows, purebred, pedigreed dogs compete for the ribbons, cups, and medals that will bring glory to their owners.

Most of all, the dog is prized as a trusting and affectionate companion. Whether highly bred or of mixed ancestry, he is a playful and appealing pet for children and a loyal friend to man.

If the photographs in this book should inspire you to require a dog, you must vow to keep him throughout his life – about twelve years – and to give him the love and attention he needs. His loyalty and devotion will be your reward. After thousands of years of living with man, dogs have earned their happiness.

Captions

Front cover: The whippet, an English breed, is a swift, temperamental dog, somewhat smaller than the greyhound, whom he resembles. *Fritz Prenzel*

1. The greyhound, the fastest dog of that breed, needs much exercise. He is reserved though friendly. *M. Scheler/Stern*
2. About half of all dachshunds in Germany are wirehairs. They make superb hunting dogs. *Monika v. Boch*
3. Children and dogs make fine companions when children are taught how to treat dogs. *Theo Frey*
4. A striking animal – the bobtail or English sheep dog. *Animal Photography*
5. Two young long-haired dachshunds. *Fritz Prenzel*
6. A tired watchdog. *Toni Schneiders*
7. Communication problems? *Othmar Herbst*
8. I'm Elke Sommer's dog. *Rudi Herzog*
9. Poodle with puppies. *Fritz Prenzel*
10. The cuddly playfulness of puppies invites affection. *Hubs Flöter*
11. A litter of wire-haired dachshunds in three pairs of socks. *Comet-Photo*
12. There is no such thing as animal friendships, but different animals can get along with each other. *Toni Schneiders*
13. This sheep dog has all the earmarks of puppyhood: woolly fur, hangdogs ears, round head. *Comet-Photo*
14. Out of the post: a Newfoundland in the role of draft animal. *Animal Photography*
15. The young Norfolk terrier feels secure in this cavelike basket. *Animal Photography*
16. Men can see through clear panes, dogs can even smell through them. *Lars W. Thieme/Pontis*
17. The power and solidity of the English bulldog are already apparent in this youngster. *Animal Photography*
18. Albergo Impero. *Theo Frey*
19. Classically trimmed poodle at play. *Animal Photography*
20. People at times behave like cats and dogs. *Paul Popper Ltd.*
21. Japan chin in Western dress. Experts say that making dogs wear coats and shoes is not only senseless but agonizing. *Paolo Koch*
22. Snowwhite from muzzle to tip of tail: a bullterrier litter, the gladiators of dogdom. *Animal Photographie*
23. The Scottish terrier on his short legs is quite a guy. *Ullstein*
24. Terriers are the British national dogs. The Airedale is the biggest of the approximately twenty terrier breeds. *Comet-Photo*
25. The basset hound is a hunting dog native to England and America which unfortunately has become a German status symbol. Bassets are two- ore three-colored. *Fritz Prenzel*
26. Mother's milk is the best (greyhound). *Paul C. Pet*
27. In the past the Dalmatian accompanied horses and coaches. His uniform and distinct markings demand knowledgeable breeders. He needs much exercise. *Fritz Prenzel*
28. The basenji is native to Africa. *Animal Photography*
29. Sheep dogs, a generic term, not a breed, see to it that herds stay together. Most of the dogs guarding the approximately 800 herds still found in Germany are sheep poodles, a no longer recognized breed. *Alfons Lutgen*
30. Dogs frequently are the only links old people have to the world around them, and the responsibility of caring for them is an important therapeutic tool. *Hubs Flöter*

31. Portrait of a smooth-haired fox terrier. *Harald Mante*
32. Not like cats and dogs. *Mario Cattaneo*
33. White poodle with classic trim. *Andy Bernhaut*
34. Mourning the loss of a faithful friend. *Roger Wrenn*
35. The most important aspect of training seeing-eye dogs is teaching them what to do, not what *not* to do. *Comet-Photo*
36. Dog cemetery. *O. v. Alphen/Pontis*
37. Almost human – Afghan hounds posing. *Animal Photography*
38. At one time Saint Bernards were used to patrol snowbound regions, but no longer. They have become to heavy and long-haired. *Comet-Photo*
39. Barry monument at the dog cemetery of Asnières near Paris. Barry, a Saint Bernard who allegedly rescued 40 people buried in the snow, has become a legend. He died in Bern, not during a rescue operation, but of old age. His body, which has been preserved, can be seen at the Museum of Natural History, Bern. *O. v. Alphen/Pontis*
40. The German sheep dog has replaced the Saint Bernard as a rescue dog. *Comet-Photo*
41. The rescue dog can pick up the scent of a person buried under a 20-foot layer of snow. *Comet-Photo*

42.–43. Barry is also the name of the dog at the mountaintop restaurant at Bad Goisern, Austria. He obviously enjoys the chair lift and knows just when to jump off. *Kurt Lorz*

44. Sled team in Greenland. *Collignon/ Black Star/O'Lear*
45. Sheep dog in the snow. *Siegfried Hartig*
46. The Ibicago, a native of Ibiza bears a remarkable resemblance to the dog gods of ancient Egypt. *Fritz Prenzel*
47. A Doberman pinscher being trained. *Animal Photography*
48. Doberman pinscher jumping a hurdle. *Animal Photography*
49. Obedience training a boxer. *Lothar Sauer*
50. Irish wolfhound, the largest of all breeds, is very rare. Needs a great deal of room and exercising. *Animal Photography*
51. Greyhounds must run; they need the exercise which racing provides. In England, greyhound races are big business, with bets running to £ 60 million per year. *Rolf G. Theissen*
52. Bloodhound on long lead. *Julius Behnke*
53. Spaniel carrying game bird. *Theo Frey*
54. Fox hunt. Riders and pack. *Hanns Hubmann*
55. Pointers. As soon as these specialists pick up the scent of game, they stand still and point out the prey to the hunter. *Animal Photography*
56. The bloodhound got its name not because of its bloodthirstiness but because of its noble bloodline. *Paul Popper Ltd.*
57. German boxer with undocked ears. *Prenzel/Mauritius*
58. Whippets as though made of china. *Animal Photography*
59. The Persian saluki, the most graceful of all hunting dogs. *Animal Photography*
60. The beagle, hunting dog and popular household pet. *Hans Jesse*
61. The Bedlington terrier, a highly intelligent dog, looks almost like a lamb. *Paul Wolff & Tritschler*
62. Start of a poodle race. *Rainer Uthoff/Pontis*
63. A victor without laurels. *Toni Schneiders*

64. Group picture of Dalmatians, women and men. *Paul Popper Ltd.*

65. Doberman pinscher Duro von Fürstenfeld, champion of champions. *Rudi Herzog*

66. Silver poodle. *Animal Photography*

67. The Labrador retriever, a fine search and water hound. *Fritz Prenzel*

68. Collies, a british breed, made favours by Lassie. *Pierre Berger*

69. Jumping through five burning hoops, more circus than true training. *Südafrikanische Botschaft, Bern*

70. Dachshund on wet street. *Riwkin*

71. The soulful look: cocker spaniels are particularly devotet. *Fritz Prenzel*

72. Poodle fisherman with dog.

73. Young fisherman with dog. *Paul Popper Ltd.*

74. Friendship. *Burr Jerger/Sirman Press*

75. The Batak Pomeranian of Asia is a prototypical domestic dog. *Barbey/Magnum/laenderpress*

76. The Lhasa Apso, a native of Tibet, is tough, alert, and lovable. *Ernest Palinkas/Hecht*

77. The large bulging eyes are symptomatic of the dwarfed breeds. The Mexican Chihuahua is the world's smallest dog. *Animal Photography*

78. Poodle standing on hind legs. *Hans Kanne*

79. Pekinese puppy sniffing flower, an idyllic picture. *Pontis*

80. No wolf can bite through the thick pelt of this Hungarian sheep dog. *Animal Photography*

Back cover: The most decorative of greyhounds, the Afghan, is as unapproachable as he looks. *Comet-Photo*

ALBERGO IMPERO
·25·

動物ホテル
ペット コンサルタント
美容・整形・犬猫結婚相談
朝9時～夜8時 日旺 祭日 午前中
TEL 361−1239

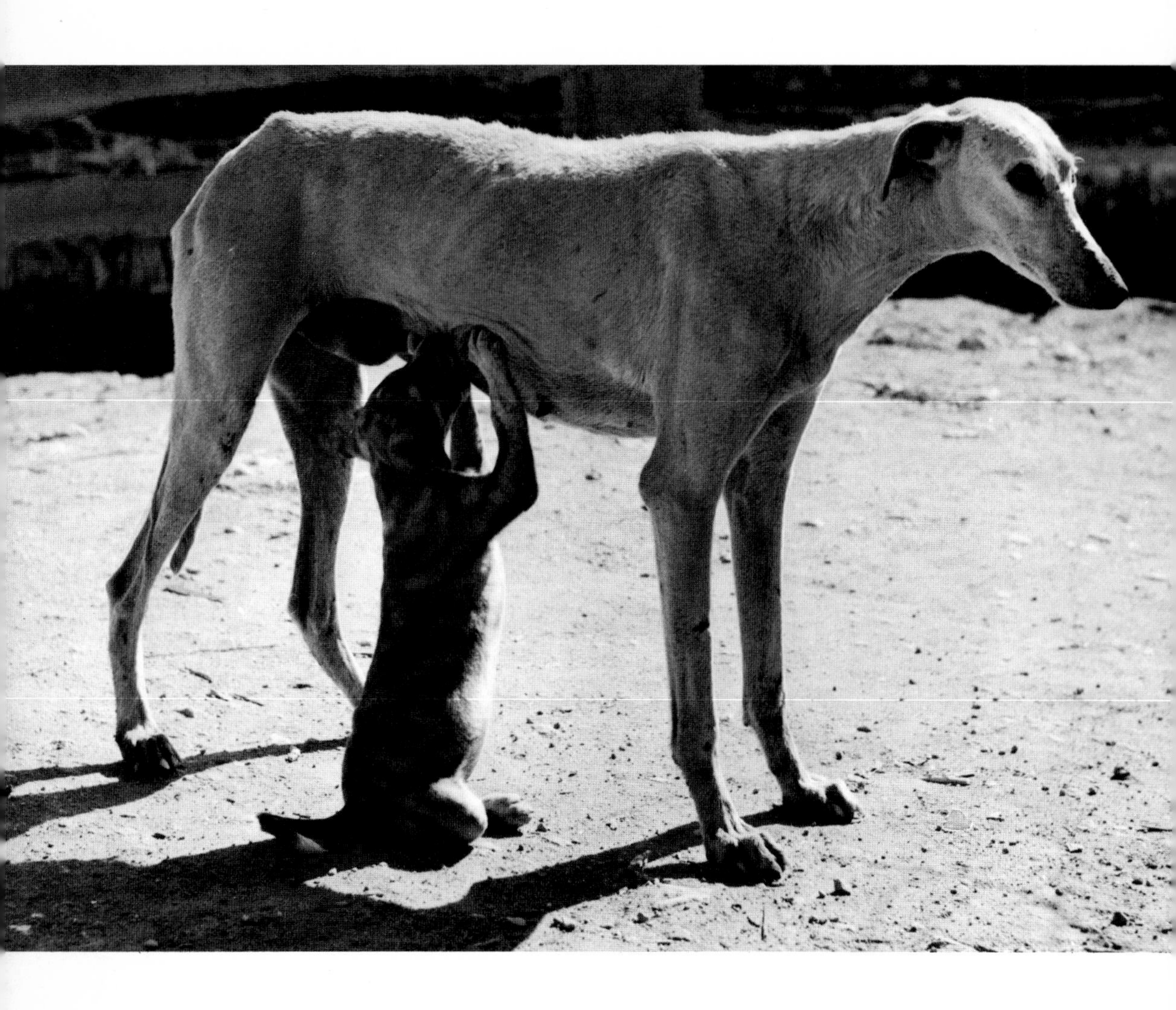

NANOU

BARRY (du Gd St Bernard)
Il sauva la vie
à 40 personnes.....
Il fût tuè par la 41ème!..

1
2

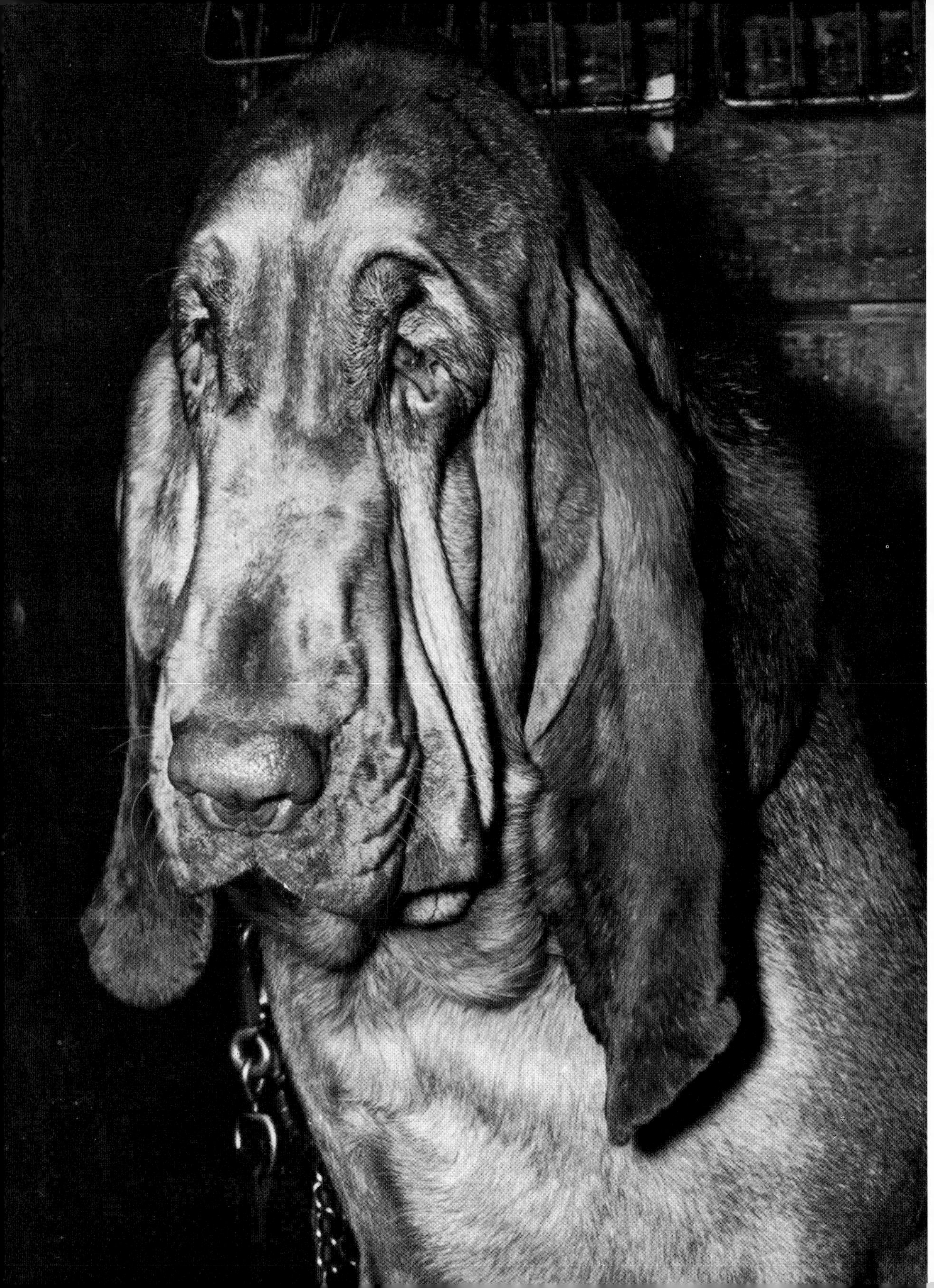

Latz füttert alle Hünde
372
VDH
IN BERLIN AM 25./26. MÄRZ 1961
CACIB
ENTE NAZIONALE DELLA CINOFILIA ITALIANA
C.A.C.I.B.
C.A.C.I.B.
C.A.C.I.B.
C.A.C.
C.A.C.
C.A.C.
C.A.C.M.
C.A.C.M.
DURO V FURSTENFELD